Games Galore!

by Beth Dvergsten Stevens

Perfection Learning®

Cover Design: Michelle Glass
Book Design: Jan M. Michalson, Lisa Lorimor

Dedication

For the kids in our neighborhood who always love a good game. With special thanks to my own children for their help and advice. May the games never end!

About the Author

Beth Stevens is a writer and former teacher. She currently writes stories and develops crafts and games for children's magazines. She also writes a weekly newspaper column for kids. Her first book, *Celebrate Christmas Around the World,* was a teacher's resource book. She has also written *Billions of Balls* and *Tops (and Other Spinning Toys)* in Perfection Learning's Cover-to-Cover Historical Toys series.

Although she's no longer in the classroom, Beth still loves teaching and learning. She hopes her readers will discover something new and interesting every time they open one of her books!

Beth lives in Waverly, Iowa, with her husband, three children, and their pets.

Image Credits
www.arttoday.com: 3, 8, 12, 61, 62; Corel Studio: 5, 6–7, 32, 49; Photodisc: cover, 14; Mike Aspengren: 15, 16, 17, 18, 35, 45; Jim Peterson: 56.

Contents

CHAPTER 1

The History of Games in the World

Have you ever played tic-tac-toe, checkers, or Monopoly? What about Go Fish or Old Maid?

Games like these have been played for thousands of years. They have been played in kings' castles and African huts. American Indians and soldiers at war have played them.

Sometimes these games were played on beautiful ivory boards. But often they were played in the dirt.

Some games had different names. Some had different rules. But people everywhere had fun playing board and card games. Today, we still play many of the same games.

Board Games

The first board games were very simple. They were just lines or holes made in the dirt.

Some lines looked like tic-tac-toe games. Others were like winding paths.

The first playing pieces were simple too. Players used rocks, shells, or nuts. They moved the pieces in the dirt.

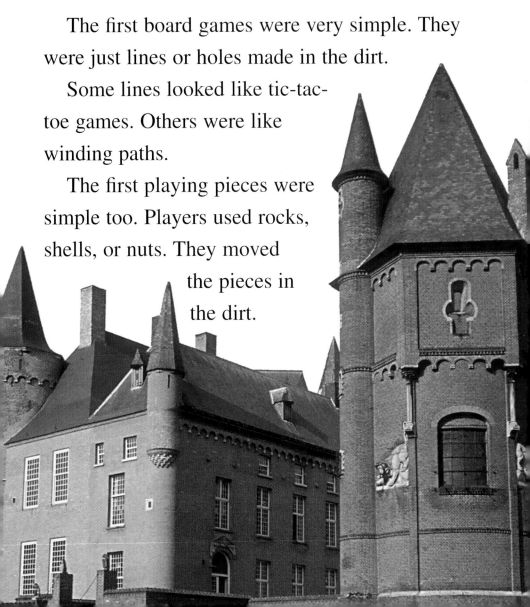

Sometimes players won. Sometimes they lost. But they always had fun!

Kings and queens played games too. But they didn't want to play in the dirt. So they hired skilled craftspeople to make fancy game boards.

Smooth game boards were carved from wood. Pretty shells or ivory decorated the boards. Polished gems became shiny game pieces.

These games were beautiful! Rulers gave board games as gifts to other kings.

Many board games were invented near Egypt. Others came from India and China. Traders and armies carried games, such as chess, to other places.

Chess was probably invented in India. Traders saw the game. They liked it. So they took it to ancient Persia and China. It reached England in the 11th century. Today, chess is played all over the world.

As time passed, people changed some of the games. They also invented wonderful new games. These games were taken to North America by the settlers.

The best games are still around. Why? Because they are fun to play. And adults have taught them to their children and grandchildren.

- The earliest board game historians know of was found in an Egyptian tomb. This game may be more than 5,000 years old! It was probably used to tell fortunes.

- An ancient mancala (man KA la) game (see page 17) was found on the roof of an Egyptian temple.

- Old game boards were found in the ruins of ancient Greece and the Roman empire. Historians think some games were used for religious ceremonies. Other games were for fun.

But we'll never know for sure how these games were used. That's because no directions were found. Historians have just made guesses from the clues they've uncovered.

Board games in the mid-1700s were made by mapmakers on paper. They colored each game by hand. It took a long time to finish one.

But these paper games tore. And they wore out quickly. So game makers put linen on the backs of the games.

Much later, games were printed on cardboard. And they were stored in boxes.

Card Games

You can play many different games with just one deck of cards. But the earliest cards didn't look like the ones we use today.

Early cards were flat sticks with special markings. These stick cards were popular in China.

As time passed, stick cards changed. The markings were printed on paper strips instead. The oldest paper card ever found was near China. It was about 1,000 years old.

Arab soldiers brought cards from China to Spain. By the late 1300s, many people in Europe were playing card games.

When Europeans came to America, so did decks of cards. How? Probably inside people's pockets!

Artists painted the earliest playing cards by hand. They used gold and silver paints.

Each deck cost a lot of money. Many people couldn't afford them.

  9

But kings and queens could buy cards. So the artists made ones that looked like the people who bought them. The faces of kings and queens were painted on the cards! These were called *face cards.*

Today's cards are printed on stiff paper. They don't cost much money. The backs have different designs. But the faces of all cards are similar. And the face cards still show kings and queens. This style of card is at least 500 years old.

Look at a deck of cards. You will see four different suits, or shapes. Spades and clubs are black. Hearts and diamonds are red. Playing cards today look like the cards used in France many years ago.

Playing Cards

Card Suits	Face Cards

Card Suits

Clubs

Diamonds

Spades

Hearts

Face Cards

King

Queen

Jack

Different countries used other shapes. Germany used acorns, bells, hearts, and leaves. Spain and Italy used batons, coins, cups, and swords.

A normal deck has 52 playing cards. There are two extra cards called jokers. Sometimes jokers are used as wild cards. That means that jokers are special.

Certain games use jokers as the highest card. Or they can be the cards worth the most points. Sometimes jokers are used in place of lost cards.

Today, a deck of cards can be found in almost every home.

CHAPTER 2

Name That Game

Board Games

Terms to Know

block or trap—to move the game pieces around the opponent's game pieces until the opponent cannot move

capture—to take another player's game piece, usually by jumping over it or trapping it

crown—to put a matching game piece on top of one that has reached the opponent's home. Crowned game pieces may move in special ways.

home—spot where the game pieces are placed at the beginning of a game. Home also can be the spot the game pieces are trying to reach.

move—taking a game piece from one spot and placing it in another. Moves are made forward, backward, sideways, or diagonally. Moves vary from game to game.

opponents—game players who are trying to beat one another

strategy—method used when players think ahead and then make smart moves

Checkers is a game from France or Spain. It's about 1,000 years old.

The French called the game *dames*. In England, it was called *draughts* (draf[t]s).

Today's game follows the same rules that were used in the 1800s. Two players try to be the first to capture or trap each other's game pieces.

Chess came from northern India. Over 1,600 years ago, it was a dice game for four people. It was called *chaturanga*. Then the game changed.

Now there are no dice. Two people play the game on a checkerboard. The game pieces have different shapes. And they move different ways. Chess is also a computer game!

Chinese checkers is a marble game. Players must move all their marbles to other players'

homes. Unlike checkers, players do not capture one another's game pieces.

Go is much older than chess. It's about 4,000 years old. But it is still very popular in China, Japan, Korea, and Taiwan. Tournaments draw people from all

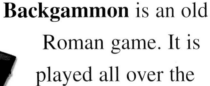

over the world. Each player uses about 180 game pieces!

Backgammon is an old Roman game. It is played all over the world. The game board is a box with hinges. Game pieces, also called *stones*, and dice are stored inside. It was often played in cafés. Maybe that's why backgammon was once called *tables*!

Mancala (often spelled *mankala*) games are very old. Rulers in Egypt played them 3,000 years ago.

Today, mancala is popular in Africa, Sri Lanka, and the West Indies.

Mancala boards have holes for the pebble game pieces. Seeds, shells, beads, or buttons can also be used. Many mancala boards are carved from wood. But the games can be played in the dirt too.

In all mancala games, players move their game pieces from one hole to the next. Each tries to win the other player's game pieces.

Mill has many other names. *Nine Men's Morris* is one of them. Players try to line up three of their game pieces at a time. That's called a *mill*.

This game began in Egypt. It has been carved into temples and furniture. It's been drawn in dirt or on sidewalks. Many mill boards are made of wood too.

Fox and geese is a simple "hunt" game. A player tries to capture or trap the opponent's game pieces.

This game has been popular in Europe since the 1400s. Other places have hunt games that are almost the same. They are called *catch the hare* and *coyote and chicken*.

Card Games

Terms to Know

book—four cards with the same number or letter. This is also called *four of a kind.*

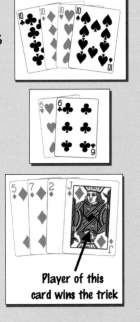

pair—two cards with the same number or letter

trick—one round of a card game, often used as a scoring unit. Each player lays down one card. The player with the highest card usually wins that round.

Player of this card wins the trick

Card games have many different rules. In each game, players do something different to win. Have you played these games?

Matching Numbers, Suits, and/or Letters

Players look for or collect cards with the same number, suit, and/or letter.

Pairs

Old Maid

concentration or memory

snap

Four of a Kind

Go Fish!

snip, snap, snorem

spoons, donkey, or pig

I doubt it

clock solitaire

go boom

my ship sails

Crazy Eights

Sequencing Games

Players put the cards in the correct number order.

card dominoes

jiggety

solitaire games (such as Klondike and golf)

Adding Games

Players do addition problems with cards.

pyramid solitaire

Speed Games

Players move cards as fast as they can!

slapjack

speed snap

spit

21

Trick-Taking Games

Players collect as many tricks as they can.

whist

linger longer

bridge

war

Solitaire card games are played by one person. They are also called *patience games*. Why? Maybe because players must be patient to win! Klondike is a familiar solitaire game.

Tips for Learning Any New Game

- Play the game while you read the directions.
- Don't worry about who wins and loses.
- Feel free to change the rules! Be sure all players agree to the changes.

Let's Play Board Games!

Getting Started

Players always take turns. But which player should go first? Here are some ideas. Choose one.

- Let the youngest or the oldest player take the first turn.
- Ask guests to go first.
- Flip a coin. The player who chooses the correct side of the coin goes first.

Checkerboard Games

A checkerboard and checkers can be used to play other games.

Checkerboard Fox and Geese

Will the fox get through?

Object of the Game

To trap the fox before he or she moves to the other side of the board

Players

 2

Needs

 1 black checker for the fox

 4 red checkers for the geese

 checkerboard

Setup

Place the checkers on the board as shown.

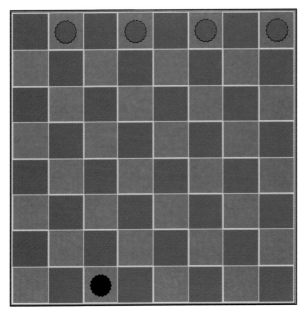

Checkerboard Fox and Geese Setup

Play

Moves are made diagonally on the black spaces, like in checkers. The fox may go backward or forward one space at a time. Geese may go forward only. There is no jumping or capturing.

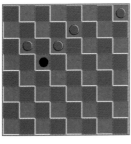

Play in progress   **Fox wins!**

Shifting Pyramids
Jump, jump, jump!

Object of the Game
To move your checkers across the board and into the opponent's home base pyramid

Players
2

Needs
10 checkers of the same color for each player

checkerboard

Setup
Place the checkers on the board as shown.

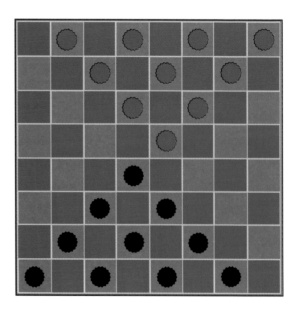

  26

Play

Moves are made diagonally on the black spaces. Players may move forward or backward one space at a time. They may also jump checkers. There is no capturing.

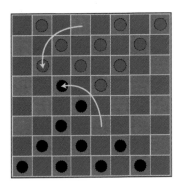 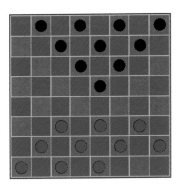

Play in progress   **Black player wins!**

Variation

Kono is a game from Korea. Set up the checkers in a U-shape instead. Play the game the same as above.

Dama
This is challenging!

Object of the Game

To capture or block the opponent's checkers until they cannot move

Players

2

Needs

12 checkers of the same color for each player

checkerboard

Setup

Cover the left- and the right-side rows of the checkerboard with paper. These rows won't be used. Players place their checkers on their own sides of the board as shown.

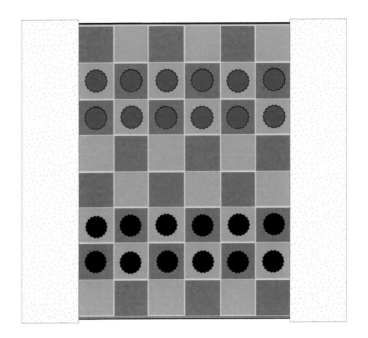

Play

Players move the checkers forward or sideways. The checkers cannot move backward or diagonally. They can jump over the opponent's checkers to capture them.

If a checker crosses the board to the opponent's last row, it is crowned king. Kings can move forward, backward, or sideways, but not diagonally. Kings can move across several empty spaces in a row to jump a checker.

Racing Board Games

Who wins a racing game? Players race, or travel, along a path. The winner must land on the last space with the exact count. If players roll numbers that would send them beyond the last space, they cannot move. They must try again on their next turn.

Try some of these racing games. Use any racing game board, such as Life. Ignore the normal rules. Play the game in new ways!

Old Game Board, New Game

Hyena Chase

Object of the Game

To be the first player to reach the finish space without being caught by the hyena

Players

2 or more

Needs

game board

1 die

1 different game piece for each player

1 game piece called the *hyena*

Setup

Place the game pieces on start. Place the hyena game piece on finish.

Play

Each player rolls the die. The player with the lowest roll is the hyena.

Players roll the die and move the game pieces toward the finish. The hyena rolls the die and moves toward the start.

To begin play and to move off the start and finish spaces, players *must* roll a 6. Then players should roll again and move ahead that number of spaces. Any time a player rolls a 6, that player gets to move and roll again.

The hyena can move either forward or backward along the path. But the hyena can only move one direction in a turn. To capture an opponent's game piece, the hyena must land on the same space as the opponent.

Players racing toward the finish can only move forward. If a game piece passes the hyena, that player is safe for that turn.

Play continues until one game piece reaches the finish or the hyena captures all the game pieces.

Old Game Board, New Rules

Use an old game board that has a start and finish. Play the game according to the rules. But try adding the following suggestions.

- Play with three or four game pieces per player. A player who lands on a space where an opponent's game piece sits sends the opponent's game piece back to the starting point. Pieces belonging to one player can sit on the same space.

- Mark three bonus spaces on the game board. Make paper shortcuts to a space ahead. A player who lands on a bonus space moves along the shortcut.

- Mark three capture spaces on the game board. A player who lands on a capture space takes any other game pieces resting on that space already.

CHAPTER 4

Let's Play Card Games!

Getting Started

Who plays? Solitaire games are played by one person. Other card games need two or more players. In some games, players have partners.

Which player deals the cards? Just as in board games, players always take turns. Deciding who should deal can be hard. Try one of these suggestions.

- Let the youngest or oldest player deal first.
- Invite a guest to deal first.
- Each player chooses one card from a deck. The player with the highest card deals first.

What is shuffling? Shuffling is a way of mixing the cards. The dealer should shuffle the cards five times before each game.

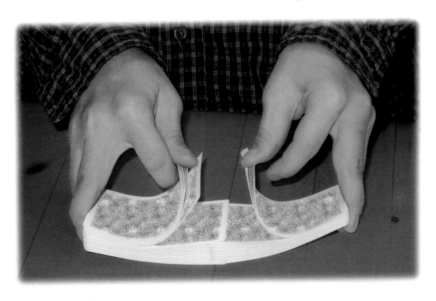

Which player takes the first turn? The player sitting on the left side of the dealer makes the first play. Play moves clockwise around the circle or table. Players take turns dealing.

Card Games for One Person

Clock Solitaire
Matching

Object of the Game

To put all four matching number cards into the correct place on the "clock" before the last king is turned up

Needs

1 deck of cards

Setup

Deal 13 piles with four cards in each pile facedown. Place 12 of the piles in a circle like the numbers on a clock. Put the last pile in the middle.

Play

Turn up the top card from the middle pile. Put it faceup under the correct number pile on the clock. Turn up the top card on that pile. Place that card under its matching pile. Continue turning up and placing cards on the clock.

Aces equal 1. Jacks equal 11. Queens equal 12. Kings equal 13 and go in the middle. When all four kings are turned up, the game is over.

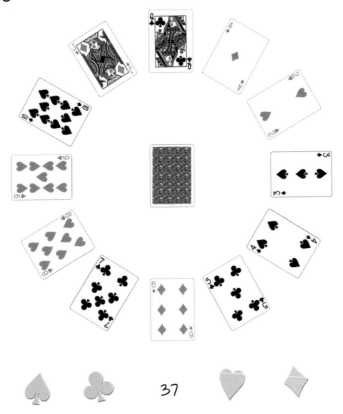

Pyramid Solitaire

Addition

Object of the Game

To make sums of 13 with pairs of cards until all the cards in the pyramid are removed

Needs

1 deck of cards

Setup

Starting at the top, make a pyramid with 28 cards faceup. Overlap the cards as you begin each new row. Only the cards in the bottom row won't have any cards on top of them. Set the rest of the cards facedown in front of you. This becomes the draw pile.

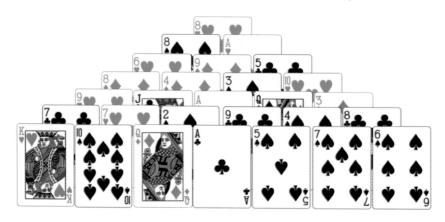

  38

Play

Turn up the top card from the draw pile. Look at its number. Can you add this number to a card from the bottom row of the pyramid to equal 13?

If so, set both cards aside. If not, place the card faceup in a discard pile. Turn up another card from the draw pile and continue.

Only pyramid cards that are completely uncovered can be used. As new cards are uncovered in the pyramid, the top card in the discard pile can be used to make 13. Kings are set aside alone.

Aces equal 1. Jacks equal 11. Queens equal 12. Kings equal 13. When you cannot make any more sums of 13, the game is over.

  39

Golf Solitaire

Sequencing

Object of the Game

To get rid of the cards from the setup

Needs

1 deck of cards

Setup

Deal five cards faceup in a row across. Make six more rows beneath the first one, overlapping the bottoms of the previous row. The rest of the cards form a draw pile.

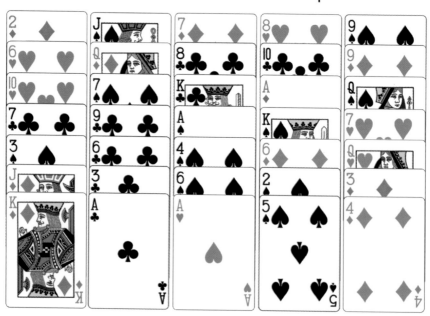

Play

Turn up one card from the draw pile. Look at the bottom row of cards. If you find a card that is one number higher or one number lower than the upturned card, take it off. Place it on the upturned card.

Check the bottom row again. One at a time, take all cards that are in sequence, up and/or down. Then turn up a new card and build another sequence.

When the draw pile is gone and you can't build more sequences, the game is over. Count the number of cards left in the setup. That's your score for this hole of golf. Play nine or eighteen holes.

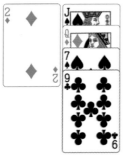

The score is 9!

41

Card Games for Two or More

War

Object of the Game

To have all the cards

Players

2 or more

Needs

1 or 2 decks of cards

Setup

Deal the cards facedown into a pile for each player. Players should not look at their cards.

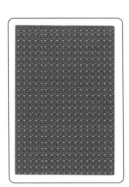

Play

Each player turns up the top card on the pile. The player with the highest card takes all the cards just played. They are placed at the bottom of the pile. If two or more players turn up cards with the same number, it's war!

Each warring player places two more cards facedown. Then the players turn up a third card. The player with the highest card takes all the cards just played. Play continues until one player has won all the cards.

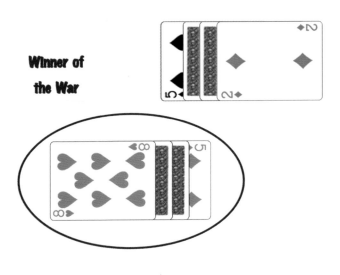

Winner of the War

Snap

Object of the Game

For one player to have all the cards

Players

2 or more

Needs

1 deck of cards

Setup

Deal cards facedown into a pile for each player. Players should not look at their cards.

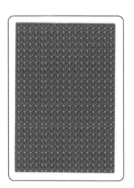

Play

Players take turns flipping up their top card one at a time. Players watch for any two cards of the same value, such as two 5s.

The first player to see two matching cards yells "Snap!" Then that player takes all the faceup cards and adds them to the bottom of his or her own pile.

Faceup piles can be turned over and played again. Play continues until one player has won all the cards.

Spoons
Also called Donkey

Object of the Game
To collect four of a kind and grab a spoon

Players
3 or more

Needs
1 deck of cards

spoons—one fewer than the number of players

Setup
Place the spoons in the middle of the table. Note: If fewer than five players are in the game, remove the 2s, 3s, 4s, and 5s from the deck.

Play
Deal four cards facedown into a pile for each player. The rest of the cards become a draw pile for the dealer. Players look at their cards

  46

and sort them by number. Cards should not be shown to the other players.

The dealer chooses a card from the draw

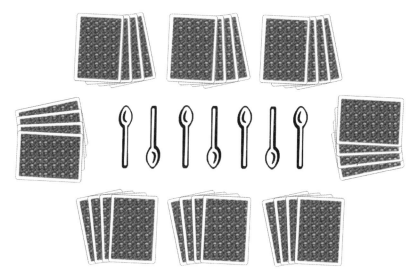

pile. The dealer can pass the card facedown to the left. Or the card can be kept. If the card is kept, a card from the dealer's hand is passed facedown to the left.

As the dealer continues to draw and discard cards, the player to the left begins by picking up the first card passed. That card is passed to the player on the left. Or it is kept and another card is passed to the left.

Play continues around the table. Players should pass the cards quickly.

When one player has four cards with the same number, that player grabs a spoon and sets the cards faceup on the table. Other players quickly grab for the remaining spoons even if they don't have four of a kind.

The player without a spoon loses that round and collects the letter D. A player who loses six times has D-O-N-K-E-Y. That player must say "hee-haw" three times.

Pig variation

Follow rules above without spoons. The winner quietly puts a finger by his or her nose. Other players copy the move as soon as they notice. The last player to notice collects the letter P. The first person with P-I-G must say "oink, oink" three times.

CHAPTER 5

Games to Make

Simple Games to Draw

Draw each game on typing
paper. Use checkers or buttons as
game pieces. Play the games
with a friend!

Well Kono

From Korea

Object of the Game

To trap the opponent's game pieces

Players

2

Needs

2 game pieces of the same color for each player

drawn game board (shown below)

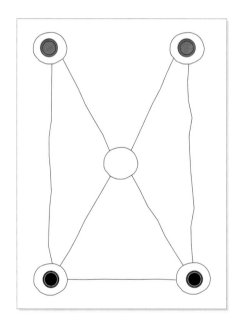

  50

Setup

Place the game pieces on the top and bottom spots as shown. Leave the center spot empty.

Play

The player with the game pieces at the top makes the first move. That player moves a game piece to an empty spot. Players then take turns moving game pieces to empty spots. All moves must follow the lines. There are no jumps.

Play continues until one player can no longer move.

Derrah

From Africa

Object of the Game

To make rows of three game pieces and capture all of the opponent's game pieces

Players

2

Needs

12 game pieces of the same color for each player

drawn game board (shown below)

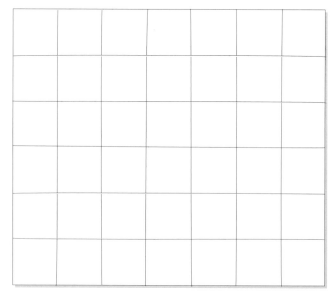

  52

Setup

Players take turns putting one game piece on the game board until all of the pieces are placed.

Play

Players take turns moving one game piece at a time to a free space. Game pieces can move any direction *except* diagonally.

Players try to put three of their own game pieces in a row in any direction. When a player makes a row of 3, that player takes one of the opponent's game pieces.

Note: Rows with four game pieces don't count. If a row of three is made when game pieces are being placed, it doesn't count either.

Game Boards to Make and Keep

Ask an adult to help you make and play these games.

Nine Men's Morris

Object of the Game
To capture all of the opponent's game pieces

Players
2

Needs

graph paper

pencil

ruler

black marker

crayons

glue stick

cardboard, such as a pizza-box lid

nine small buttons of the same color for each player

Steps

1. On graph paper, draw a 6-inch square. Draw a 4-inch square centered inside it. Then draw a 2-inch square in the middle.

2. Draw a short line from the center square,

through the middle of each side, to the outside line.

3. Trace the lines with a dark marker. Draw a small circle at each point where two lines meet.

4. Color the squares.

5. Glue the game to a piece of cardboard, such as a pizza-box lid.

Play

Players take turns putting one game piece anywhere on the gameboard until all pieces are placed. They try to place three of their game pieces in a row. Each player tries to block the other player from getting three in a row.

When all game pieces are placed, players move a game piece one space per turn. Moves must follow lines. There is no jumping. When a player makes a row of three, that player takes one game piece from the opponent. The game ends when one player cannot move or has only two markers left.

  55

Basic Chase or Race Game Board

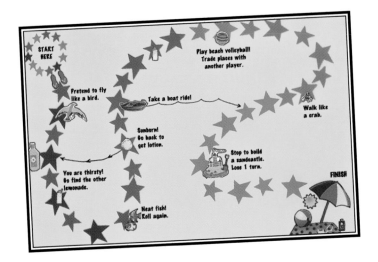

Object of the Game

To be the first player to land on the finish space

Players

2 or more

Needs

pencil or markers
construction paper
stickers
1 different game piece for each player
die

  56

Steps

1. Choose a theme and stickers.

2. Draw starting and ending spaces on construction paper. Draw a winding path between the spaces.

3. Place stickers along path, about one inch apart to create playing spaces.

4. Every three to six spaces, write a hazard or bonus instruction.

   Hazard examples include *lose 1 turn* and *go back 3 spaces*. Bonus examples include *take an extra turn, jump ahead 3 spaces*, and *take a shortcut*.

   Other fun spaces include *trade places with another player, go to another space,* and *stand up and do something silly*.

5. Decorate the game board.

Play

Each player chooses a game piece. Players take turns. The first player rolls the die. That player moves his or her game piece ahead the number of spaces shown on the die. Play continues until one player reaches the finish.

All players landing on a bonus or hazard space must follow the instructions for that space.

CHAPTER 6

Great Game Trivia

Crazy Card and Game Facts

- Old cards from Asian countries were often round.

- Not all playing cards are paper. Some are made from metal, leather, or thin pieces of wood. There are even cards made from stiff fabric, ivory, and shell!

- In the United States, there are more than 250 billion decks of cards.

- In colonial America, people had to buy games from England. They had to pay taxes on them too. Some Americans didn't like that. So they made their own cards. But if the Americans were caught with these non-English cards, they had to pay fines!

- Some people collect playing cards. They look for special decks with interesting pictures on the back.

- What's a squeezer? Long ago, the marks on cards were printed only in the middle. Then a card maker from England invented the *squeezer*. These cards had marks in two corners of each card. Players could "squeeze" their cards close together. Then they could still see which cards they held!

- Great game inventions include game pieces and cards that have been marked for people who are visually impaired.

They can feel the raised marks with their fingers. Then they can play games and cards too.

- When gaslights were invented in the early 1800s, people started playing more games. Why? Their homes were bright inside. They could stay up later at night. They spent their extra time playing games!

A large-scale chess game on Antigua island in the Caribbean

Did You Know?

- Ancient chess pieces looked like chariots, elephants, horsemen, and foot soldiers.

- Shepherds in England cut game boards into the grass. Then they played Nine Men's Morris. The shepherds themselves were the game pieces!

- In Japan, some game players are professionals. They go to special schools to learn how to play well.

- Many different countries had "hunt" board games. Why? Because in real life, strong animals hunted weaker ones. Board games copied real life.

What Did You Say?

Common Phrases from Games

Poker Face

This is a blank look you keep on your face so your opponents won't know what you're thinking. In cards, a poker face is important. Then other players won't know if you have winning or losing cards.

The Luck of the Draw

This means to have good luck in something. In cards, it is when players pick the right card and win by pure chance, or luck.

Close to the Vest

This is when someone keeps information secret. Card players hold their cards close to their bodies. Then other players can't see them.

Roll of the Dice

This is when someone takes a chance on something good or bad. When players roll the dice, they never know what they'll get!

Card "Games" and Tricks

Card Sailing

Use old cards. Flip each card like a Frisbee. Make it spin and fly across a room. Good card sailors make the cards return to their hands. Cards are just like boomerangs!

House of Cards

Use old cards. Build lots of teepees with two cards for each one. Then lay other cards on top of the teepees like flat roofs. Add more layers of teepees and roofs. Build the tallest card houses you can!

52 Pickup

This is a trick to play with fun-loving friends. Ask them if they want to play 52 pickup. If they say yes, throw a deck of cards into the air. Then say, "Now we pick them up—all 52 of them!" Be sure you help too.